Diary Rooms

Being human on the front line in Afghanistan

big
ideas
library

Diary Rooms

Being human on the front line in Afghanistan

Derek Eland

Published by The Big Ideas Library

First published in Great Britain
First edition 2014

ISBN 978-0-9929859-0-5

Designed by Ned Hoste, The Big Ideas Collective
Printed by CPI Group (UK)

Praise for the Diary Rooms project

'Groundbreaking' *The Independent*

'Raw, poignant' *The Mirror*

'Staggering' *The Huffington Post*

'Emotionally charged' *Agence France-Presse*

'Poignant and personal' *The BBC*

'Extraordinary' *CNN*

'Fascinating, and moving'
   Jennifer Higgie, Editor, *frieze magazine*

'Incredibly compelling. An immense emotive encounter'
   Middlesbrough Institute of Modern Art

Shortlisted for the Museums and Heritage Awards
for Excellence 2014

Dedication

David Dalzell
Colum McGeown

Contents

Introduction

When I was first given the chance to become a war artist in Afghanistan it was a question of how to bring a new perspective to the conflict; one dominated by the relentless toll of deaths and the hyper-reality of the head-cam videos. I wanted to get inside the heads of people in this war zone to find out what it feels like to 'be human' in this demanding place.

In a digital age, when people don't write any more, I decided to collect handwritten stories on the front line. I didn't want stories written after the event; I was interested in honest, raw and immediate accounts, written there and then. I asked everyone I met on the front line, Afghan soldiers and interpreters and Westerners, to write a postcard about what it was like to be there. These stories were collated in three Big Brother-style 'Diary Rooms' in Helmand, Afghanistan.

'Diary Room',
Patrol Base Kalang,
Afghanistan,
2011

The Diary Rooms were located in the most 'kinetic' areas. This is military speak for places where the fighting with the Taliban was most intense, as it was thought that the people I met would have more interesting stories to tell. The majority of soldiers were dotted around the landscape in small check points and on day two in Helmand I left the relatively safe confines of the larger bases to patrol out to these remote locations. This meant that I was immediately on the same level as the soldiers – I patrolled with them, slept in these remote places and took the same risks – and could 'ask' them for their stories. Quite often when I turned up in these remote locations they would initially ask where my easel and paints were but they quickly understood and got on with writing their stories. My initial worry that soldiers would only write what they thought others wanted them to say or that they would not write anything at all was unfounded.

Derek Eland with the Royal Irish Regiment, Afghanistan, 2011

Why did people write their stories so readily? I gave the soldiers a relatively short time to write to ensure the stories were not too reflective and also because I had only a limited time on the ground in some of these places. I soon realised that the stories were startlingly honest and insightful. They were not things they would tell their families back home because it would worry them too much. Equally, they were things that the soldiers wouldn't tell each other because they were often highly personal and they might betray weakness. The stories ranged from the remarkable to the mundane, the extraordinary to the everyday.

These were intense places. I was with the Royal Irish Regiment in a small location which had been involved in 87 shootings and bombings with the Taliban in three months. I worked with soldiers from the Parachute Regiment who were guarding and clearing an empty village of IEDs to enable Afghan families to move back into their homes. With the Irish Guards in the north at Khar Nikah we were attacked one night from multiple firing points. I noticed in all these situations where I also filmed and photographed the soldiers at work that they fought with the same intensity with which they wrote their stories.

What was the end result? The Diary Rooms filled up, hundreds of stories were written, mostly on coloured cards, but sometimes on scraps of paper, cardboard ripped from ration boxes or scribbled on blank medical forms. One soldier took an empty packet of sliced pears and wrote 'Yummy' on the side. A female medic wrote what it was like to treat her first casualties and save their lives, a chef described cooking and distributing Christmas dinner to hundreds of soldiers scattered about the front line, a bomb disposal expert described what it felt like to go to Afghanistan as a battle casualty replacement for someone who had been injured. Some of those who wrote stories went on to be killed or seriously wounded. In these cases the families concerned have given permission for the stories to be published.

'Diary Room', Forward Operating Base,
Khar Nikah, Afghanistan, 2011

The overall response I got was staggering and included excerpts such as:

"Your mind clicks into a gear that you never knew you had, and you bark orders like your life depends on it... and GUESS WHAT: IT DOES!"

"My abiding memory of Afghanistan? ...it will be a humble local farmer who one day took me by surprise by asking after my family. "You are far from home. You must miss you family very much. We are very grateful.""

"The young soldier was brought to me following an IED blast...I didn't need to ask more questions – his eyes told the whole story; as wide open as possible and conveying such a sense of bewilderment, uncertainty and terror that I shall never forget them."

'Diary Room', Patrol Base 1,
Afghanistan, 2011

"I'm going to write about the day-to-day struggle of being away... what your girlfriend was wearing last time you saw her, what she did, said, what she smelt like, what she will look like and if anything will have changed while you have been away, and if you will fit in with the changes when you get back... if you are close to someone that is away out here, know that you will always be in their minds because there are two wars being fought, one which is publicised and one which goes on in a soldier's head when everything goes quiet..."

What evolved became an enormous self-portrait.
Their stories.

Derek Eland, June 2014

"To the World he
was a Soldier…

to us he was the World"

David Dalzell's story p93

Our son Ranger David Gordon Dalzell served with 1st Battalion Royal Irish Regiment and was fatally shot at Camp Ranger, Nad-e-Ali district, Afghanistan at 0603 on 4th February 2011.

Our definition of normal changed forever that day. It is and continues to be filled with disbelief and despair.

What makes this so very tragic is that David was accidently shot by his best friend, Sean. They met at Catterick Army Training Centre, trained together and passed out beside each other. They deployed together to Afghanistan serving beside each other at Camp Ranger where some of the fiercest fighting took place. Following our recent meeting with Derek Eland we watched footage he had taken of David and Sean together on patrol and for that we are extremely grateful.

David was our youngest son and was the most gorgeous, happy child who grew up to be an equally gorgeous and happy young man. He was surrounded by love; his smile would melt his father's and my heart. He had an infectious laugh and a wicked sense of humour but was incredibly loyal and protective of his family.

We were immensely proud of David when he passed out after training in July 2010.

Having been informed that David had been shot by a fellow soldier and having limited factual information, we could not make sense of what had happened. Physically and emotionally we were shut down, devoid, numb. It was only when Reverend Andrew Totten returned from Afghanistan that we got a clear and concise account of events. It was then that we realised how close a bond Sean and David had.

In May 2011, 16 weeks after David's death, Gordon and I met Sean. Gordon recounts this memory as being frightened – -frightened of his reaction towards Sean; of anger, hatred that this person had killed our son. However when face to face you realise that he too is just a young boy with a mum, dad and family that must be so worried about him and that it was an accident. He spoke about his friendship with David and his genuine regret at what had happened. Following this meeting we felt relief.

We were made aware of court-martial proceedings against Sean and decided to speak on his behalf, asking the court to show Sean leniency so he could continue his military career and in doing so, in David's name also.

My view now is that if David was to be killed in Afghanistan that I am grateful it was by Sean. No-one pointed a gun in hatred at our son and wished him dead, he wasn't blown up by an IED. It was a tragic accident. We were able to see David the day after his repatriation back to the UK. He was beautiful, he was perfect.

Gordon and I now refer to life as before David's death and life after David's death but will remain immensely proud of David, the man he became and what he achieved in his short life and that he was a soldier in such a distinguished Regiment.

We feel honoured that Derek asked us to write about our son. Reading the messages on the postcards, you get a snapshot into the lives of the soldiers on the frontline and we feel privileged to read their thoughts, some very funny and others so heartfelt, moving and so profoundly sad.

Losing David, we as parents lost part of our identity; his death has subtracted from who we were, creating a new identity for us that will last a lifetime.

Susan Dalzell
May 2014

"All gave some, some gave all"

The Stories

Every day a bang happens

EVERY DAY A BANG HAPPENS
some small, some Large,
some so Big it shakes you
in your Bed. I didn't know
which Bang was the one
which blew my mates Legs
Off. SAD DAY, in shock for
most of it. On the ground,
Few days Later going to
Live in Afghans Compounds,
one next to two Craters
with Med Kit scattered
around the scene, plus Blown
off pieces of uniform in
trees. 4 months until I
can celebrate surviving,
Alot of Brews to drink
too. Pte MAXFIELD 2 PARA

b.

EVERY DAY A BANG HAPPENS.
Some small, some Large,
Some so Big it SHAKES you
in your Bed. I didnt know
which BANG WAS the one
which blew my mates Legs
Off. SAD DAY, in shock for
most of it. On the ground,
Few days later going to
live in Afghans compounds,
One next to two Craters
with med kit scattered
around the Scene, Plus BLown
Off pieces of uniform in
trees. 4 months until I
can celebrate surviving,
Alot of Brews to drink
too. Pte MAYFIELD 2 PARA

We are on borrowed time

This tour has been a sobering
and maturing experience. Its
certainly increased the wrinkles
and creases in my face
which has resulted in me
lookin 28 and im 20.
Most of all its made me appreciate
the little things that we take
for granted.
I miss my girlfriend
and small things like driving my
car or going to the shops.
Its made me appreciate hard work
and changed my train of
thought and my view of life
and death completely.
We are on borrowed time,
so use it wisely!!
BIG MIKE
AIRBORNE!!

This tour has been a sobering
ty and maturing experience. Its
certainley increased the whrinkles
and li creases in my face
which has resulted in me
lookin 28 and im 20.
Most of all its made me appreciate
the little things that we take
for granted.
I miss my girlfriend :(

and small things like driving my
car or going to the shops.

Its made me appreciate hard work
and changed my train of
thought and my view of life ::
and death completely
We are on borrowed time,
so use it wisely !!

BIG MIKE

AIRBORNE !!

I miss home. Never again!

I Miss home!

Never again!

The tears were streaming down my face

16 Medical Regt

26/01/11
This is my Second tour of
Afghan in the past two
years.
Herrick 8 was an easy tour
for me.
Herrick 13 has been such an
experience for me.
As a female medic being in
the Army is hard enough.
Ive worked with Irish Guards,
2 coy for over 3 months
now, the lads are a great
bunch, and coz of them,
its making my tour go
fast.
On November 7th 2010

some of the Lads were on
Patrol just outside of
BDR, myself and some of
5 plt lads were QRF.
At about 06:35 we heard
an explosion, (IED) so we
got crashed out, as I knew
we had a casualty, to be
honest my mind just
blocked out what was
going on, my heart was
racing… as we came to
meet 4 plt and the other
Lads, there ■■■■ was double
amp to both Legs, we put
him onto the tallon stretcher
and I done my checks on
the move, as we got back

some of the Lads were on
Patrol just outside of
BDR, myself and some of
5plt lads were QRF.
At about 06:35 we heard
an explosion, (IED) so we
got crashed out, as i Knew
we had a casualty, to be
honest my mind just
blocked out what was
going on, my heart was
racing… as we came to
meet 4plt and the other
Lads, there ██ was double
amp to both Legs, we put
him onto the tallon Stretcha
and I done my checks on
the move, as we got back

to Bdr, after the great CASEVAC from the lads, I began to continue my treatment, For myself ████ was my First actual casualty and all I thought of doing was saving his life. ████ was so calm and to be honest he made all of us calm. I asked if he needed anything.. he said a fag, So big Jim gave him one while Rob was sending the mist report. Shortly after the heli came in to pick ████ up, we all went back into the PB. Of course the anger, sadness and feelings were all over the place.

I went over to sort out my med kit, then one of the Plt Sgts shouted on me "Sully", So I went over, he gave me a hug and the tears were streaming down my face, at that point that's when I thought how fast it can happen to people.

Shortly after, all we heard was, right Lads, kit on, use have 5 mins, then we were back out, I looked at Bish and Jerry, without saying a word, we knew exactly what we were thinking.

To this day I will never Forget the 7th Nov 2010.

More stars than you possibly imagined

JUST OF STAG, FIRING ILLUME FOR
TALIBAN AND MINI FLARES AT BARKING
DOGS. LOOKING AT THE UNPOLLUTED SKY AT
NIGHT, MORE STARS THAN YOU POSSIBLY
IMAGINED, LIVING IN LONDON OFFERS LITTLE IN
THAT RESPECT, R+R IN JUST OVER 2 WEEKS,
GOTTA STAY STRONG, FOCUSED, SWITCHED ON,
SKILLS AND DRILLS GOT TO BE PERFECT, KEEP
FIGHTING, OUT-THINK THEM, OUT-SMART THEM,
OUT-WORK THEM. ■■■■ MY LOVE I'LL
SEE YOU AT BRIZE IN 2 ½ WEEKS.
GDSM McGEOWN 1ST BATTALION IRISH GUARDS

JUST OF STAG, FIRING ILLUME FOR
TALIBAN AND MINI FLARES AT BARKING
DOGS. LOOKING AT THE UNPOLLUTED SKY AT
NIGHT, MORE STARS THAN YOU POSSIBLY
IMAGINED, LIVING IN LONDON OFFERS LITTLE IN
THAT RESPECT, R+R IN JUST OVER 2 WEEKS,
GOTTA STAY STRONG, FOCUSED, SWITCHED ON,
SKILLS AND DRILLS GOT BE PERFECT, KEEP
FIGHTING, OUT-THINK THEM, OUT-SMART THEM,
OUT-WORK THEM. ████████ MY LOVE I'LL
SEE YOU AT BRIZE IN 2 ½ WEEKS.
        GDSM McGEOWN   1ST BATTALION
                              IRISH GUARDS

One of the bravest me I ever knew

3/2/11   2 COY

TO GDSM McGEOWN, 1ST BATTALION IRISH GUARDS
SORRY IT HAD TO BE
YOU MUCKER "G". NOW YOU CAN BE WITH
YOUR LOVE AND BABY AND NEVER
COME BACK TO THIS HELL HOLE!
       SEE YOU SOON, STAY STRONG
ONE OF THE BRAVEST MEN I KNOW. FACT!
LCPL BROWNLOW (MEDIC)   (HERO)

3/2/11

<u>2 COY</u>

TO   GDSM McGEOWN, 1ST BATTALION IRISH
GUARDS

SORRY   IT HAD TO BE

YOU <u>MULKER "G"</u>. NOW YOU CAN BE WITH

YOUR   LOVE ♡ AND BABY AND NEVER

COME BACK TO THIS HELL HOLE!

SEE YOU SOON, STAY STRONG

ONE OF THE BRAVEST MEN I KNOW, <u>FACT</u>!

(HERO)

LCPL BROWNLOW (MEDIC)

35

Come and protect Afghans

I want to say for the
young boys to come –
and join ANA –
and protect Afghans

صفحم

زما وینا دافغانستان
لمولوکړ ا نافوسته داد،ڼی

د خپل ملی ارد و ننه واسی او ده
ملی ار کیکو ننه را و دائی او خپل

هیواد نته مسوله او د راښت

را ولي زه دفغانستان جو ه دم خپل یوسان تومم

37

One of the coolest days of my life

My first contact was very exciting and scary at the same time the rounds cracked over my head and landed in fround of me they kicked up dust I new they were close all I wanted to do was make sure my mates were ok I had a look every one was fine then I started Fireing my weapon I the enemys direction then mortars came in the ground shook It was one of the coolest days. of my life.

My first contact was very exciting and scary at the same time the rounds cracked over my head and landed in frount of me they kicked up dust I new they were close all I wanted to do was make sure my mates were oh I had a look every one was fine then I started fireing a my weapon I the enemys direction then mortors came in the ground shouck it was one of the coolesd days. of my life.

Wish you were here

Dear Mum,
Weather lovely   My Mum
Locals friendly   The UK

Food fantastic

Wish you were here   Tom x
                      2 PARA

All I want to do is get back to my warm kennel

All I WANT TO
Do IS GET BACK
TO MY WARM
IKENNEL

EYAN (WOOF)

Protection dog

Responsibility

Responsibility

THE SNIPER WITH A MAN IN HIS
SIGHTS: "CAN I FIRE"?

WATCH A MAN BLOWN THREE METRES
INTO THE AIR ON A ROUTE YOU SELECTED.

SEE A MAN SHOT ON A ROOF YOU ORDERED
HIM TO OCCUPY.

THIS AFGHAN WANTS MY TRUST BUT THE
TALIBAN WILL KILL HIM FOR IT.

TO HOLD A MAN'S INNOCENCE, HIS SANITY,
HIS LIFE, HIS FUTURE IN YOUR HANDS.

SORRY CHRIS…
AND ALL THE OTHERS WHO
HAVE SUFFERED.

I DID MY BEST.

QUIS SEPARABIT   AN OFFICER.

RESPONSIBILITY

THE SNIPER WITH A MAN IN HIS
    SIGHTS : " CAN I FIRE " ?

WATCH A MAN BLOWN THREE METRES
  INTO THE AIR ON A ROUTE YOU SELECTED.

SEE A MAN SHOT ON A ROOF YOU ORDERED
    HIM TO OCCUPY.

THIS AFGHAN WANTS MY TRUST BUT THE
  TALIBAN WILL KILL HIM FOR IT.

TO HOLD A MAN'S INNOCENCE, HIS SANITY,
      HIS LIFE, HIS FUTURE IN YOUR HANDS.

SORRY CHRIS...
AND ALL THE OTHERS WHO
HAVE SUFFERED.
I DID MY BEST.

QUIS SEPARABIT.   AN OFFICER.

To an officer

Your BEST Is More than Good
enough. We would follow you
to the Gates of hell and back.

A Soldier

QS

_____

VERY MUCH SECONDED.
YOU SHARE THE SAME RISKS WITH
A SEEMINGLY INFINITE CALMNESS
VERY PROUD TO HAVE SERVED UNDER
YOU.

To An Officer,

Your Best Is More than Good
enough. We would follow you
to the Gates of hell and back.

A Soldier

QS

VERY MUCH SECONDED.
You SHARE THE SAME RISKS WITH
A SEEMINGLY INFINITE CALMNESS.
VERY PROUD TO HAVE SERVED UNDER
You.

And they still steal our shovels

I could never Really understand
The afghan people in NAD 'E' ali
we build new schools, new Roads
we put money back into there community,
Provide security against the taliban
and they still steal our shovels

I could never Really understand
The afghan people in NAD E'ali.
we build new schools, new Roads
we put money back into there community
Proide security against The taliban
and they still steal our shovels

Two wars

The thing that im going to write about is something that is never portrayed in the press or anywhere i have ever seen, Its not a war story where rounds are landing everywhere or on the other hand it isnt a daily log, It is something that all people dont understand until you have been somewhere like this for this amount of time. Im going to write about the day to day struggle of being away. When people think of being in Afghanistan i think they instantly think of soldiers being shot at and bombs landing around people, and while those things happen daily those are the things that you came here for, you came here to fight a war. On the other side the thoughts of the people you miss and the things you miss and the thoughts you have about this, when you aren't out fighting or keeping yourself busy this is what is constantly going through your head. What your girlfriend was wearing last time you saw her, what she did, said, what she

and bombs landing around people, and while
those things happen daily those are the things
that you came here for, you came here to fight
a war. On the other side the thoughts of
the people you miss and the things you miss
and the thoughts you have about this, when you
aren't out fighting or keeping yourself
busy this is what is constantly going through
your head. What your girlfriend was wearing last
time you saw her, what she did, said, what she

smelt like, what she will look like and if
anything will have changed while you have been away
and if you will fit in with the changes when you
get back. I sit here and miss just fitting into
the daily routine at home, sleeping in a normal bed,
seeing all the people you love, seeing your home, sitting
down and relaxing. Sometimes it drives you crazy missing
everything and sometimes it makes you smile knowing
that you will have those things to look forward
to again. As I said at the start yes we are

smelt like, what she will look like and if
anything will have changed while you have been away
and if you will fit in with the changes when you
get back. I sit here and miss just fitting into
the daily routine at home, sleeping in a normal bed
seeing all the people you love, seeing your home, sitting
down and relaxing. Sometimes it drives you crazy missing
everything and sometimes it makes you smile knowing
that you will have those things to look forward
to again. As I said at the start yes we are

over here fighting a war and yes bad things
are constantly happeing out here but take away
with you something else when you read this, hold
onto the people you love and the things that you
love doing. If you are close to someone that is
away out here know that you will always be in
their minds because their are two wars being faught,
one which is publicised and one which goes on
in a soldiers head when everything goes quiet....
Written by a soldier with A Coy 1 Royal Irish.

over here fighting a war and yes bad things
are constantly happeing out here but take away
with you something else when you read this, hold
onto the people you love and the things that you
love doing. If you are close to someone that is
away out here know that you will always be in
their minds because their are two wars being faught,
one which is publicised and one which goes on
in a soldiers head when everything goes quiet....
Written by a soldier with A Coy 1 Royal Irish

I did what others did not want to do

I am that which others did not want to be,
I did what others did not want to do,
and went where others feared to go,
I have felt the blistering cold,
stared death in the face,
and enjoyed only a moments Love,

Even tho no one cares who i am or what i've done,
I can honestly say
I am proud of what i am!
    A SOLDIER

I am that which others did not want to be,
I did what others did not want to do,
and went where others feared to go,
I have felt the blistering cold,
stared death in the face,
and enjoyed only a moments love,

Even tho no one cares who i am or what i've done,
I can honestly say
I am proud of what i am!
 <u>A SOLDIER</u>

Is he still alive, he is still alive

December 30th 2010

On R+R at my mother in laws for dinner, I get a phone call from a good mate saying have you heard have I heard what with a sinking feeling going through my body. Its ■■■■ he has been hurt, he's a Cat A he's been shot. How bad is he is he still alive, he is still alive. The Coy had done a heli assault into Dactran he was working as the 2i/c of C/S C34 in a outer cordon when he got hit.

The feeling of a good mate getting hurt, while I was on R+R was gutting I wanted to be there with them my mates.

Cpl TOGWELL

2 Para

December 30th 2010

On R+R at my mother in laws for dinner, I get a phone call from a good mate saying have you heard have I heard what with a sinking feeling going through my body. Its ██████ he has been hurt, he's a cat A he's been shot. How bad is he is he still alive, he is still alive. The Coy had done a heli assault into Doctran he was working as the 2ic of C/S C34 in a outter Cordon when he got hit.

The feeling of a good mate getting hurt, while I was on R+R was gutting I wanted to be there with them my mates.

Cpl TOGWELL
2 Para.

What worries me is losing a bloke

I am a Combat Medic Technician attached to 1 Royal Irish.

As a medic, every time I am about to go On patrol or op, I always panic as to whether I got enough resources and well prepared to treat the casualty if I get any, and I always say silent prayers to God for protection that my call sign should return in one piece with no injuries. On this tour, I have been lucky comparing to my fellow medics as I only have had Gun shot wounds so far and are easy to treat.

I am a Combat Medic
Technician attached to
1 Royal Irish.
As a medic, every time
I am about to go on patrol or
op, I always panic as to
whether I got enough resources
and well prepared to treat the
casualty if I get any, and
I always say silent prayers
to God for protection that my
call sign should return in
one piece with no injuries.
One this tour, I have been lucky
comparing to my fellow medics
as I only have had Gun shot
wounds so far and are easy to
treat.

However I continue
praying that none of the
people I am providing
medical cover for, don't
get injured or at least not
serious Injuries.
My mind will be at rest
when I return home and
live a normal life without
worrying of getting casualties.
The contact or getting shot
doesn't worry me, what worries
me is loosing a bloke becoz
I couldn't save him.
However, I don't doubt my
medical skills, I believe to
be a better medic and good at
my job.

So many stories etched on their tired faces

SO MANY STORIES ETCHED ON
THEIR TIRED FACES FROM THESE
PAST 5 MONTHS IN HELMAND.
THEY LOOKED AFTER ME WELL
AND LOVED 'CHARM' MY MWD
(MILITARY WORKING DOG) THE MOST
PHOTOGRAPHED DOG IN NATO,
I WAS PLEASED HE BROUGHT
A LOT OF MUCH NEEDED MORAL
TO A LOT OF THE LADS.
I DON'T KNOW WHY WERE HERE
BUT ALL THESE LADS ARE REAL
HEROES, THEY DO THESE JOB WITHOUT
QUESTION AND PROFFESSIONAL.
SOON BE HOME TIME FOR ME AND
THEM AND IT WILL BE A WELOME
HOME FOR EVERYONE OF THEM.
    LCPL & MWD CHARM.
        TMWDSU BASTION

SO MANY STORIES ETCHED ON
THEIR TIRED FACES FROM THERE
PAST 5 MONTHS IN HELMAND.
THEY LOOKED AFTER ME WELL
AND LOVED 'CHARM' MY MWD
(MILITARY WORKING DOG) THE MOST
PHOTOGRAPHED DOG IN NATO,
I WAS PLEASED HE BROUGHT
A LOT OF MUCH NEEDED MORAL
TO A LOT OF THE LADS.
I DON'T KNOW WHY WERE HERE
BUT ALL THESE LADS ARE REAL
HEROES, THEY DO THERE JOB WITHOUT
QUESTION AND PROFFESIONAL.
SOON BE HOME TIME FOR ME AND
THEM AND IT WILL BE A WELCOME
HOME FOR EVERYONE OF THEM.
        LCPL & MWD CHARM.
        TMWDSU BASTION.

Love the life you live, live the life you love

IT WAS MY FIRST TOUR OF AFGHAN
AND UPON ARRIVING I HAD MIXED
FEELINGS OF BOTH NERVES AND
EXCITEMENT FOR WHAT WAS
WAITING FOR ME WITHIN THE
NEXT 6 MONTHS. I WAS SETTLING
IN AND ADJUSTING NICELY TO
THE CONDITIONS WHEN I CAUGHT
DRIFT OF SOME NEWS THAT WAS
TO CHANGE THE WAY I THOUGHT
OF LIFE. IT WAS 3 DAYS IN WHEN
I HEARD OF MATTHEW THOMAS
BEING CAUGHT IN AN IED AND
SADLY PASSING, HE WAS A GREAT
BLOKE WHO TOOK LIFE AND MADE
THE MOST OF IT A TRUE PROFESSIONAL
WHO I'D KNOWN AND SERVED WITH
FOR OVER 2YRS I THINK EVEN TO
THIS DAY I HAVENT DEALT WITH IT
EVEN WITH OTHER ACCOUNTS OF

IT WAS MY FIRST TOUR OF AFGHAN
AND UPON ARRIVING I HAD MIXED
FEELINGS OF BOTH NERVES AND
EXCITEMENT FOR WHAT WAS
WAITING FOR ME WITHIN THE
NEXT 6 MONTHS. I WAS SETTLING
IN AND ADJUSTING NICELY TO
THE CONDITIONS WHEN I CAUGHT
DRIFT OF SOME NEWS THAT WAS
TO CHANGE THE WAY I THOUGHT
OF LIFE. IT WAS 3 DAYS IN WHEN
I HEARD OF MATTHEW THOMAS
BEING CAUGHT IN AN IED AND
SADLY PASSING, HE WAS A GREAT
BLOKE WHO TOOK LIFE AND MADE
THE MOST OF IT A TRUE PROFESSIONAL
WHO I'D KNOWN AND SERVED WITH
FOR OVER 2YRS I THINK EVEN TO
THIS DAY I HAVEN'T DEALT WITH IT
EVEN WITH OTHER ACCOUNTS OF

OF FRIENDS AND COLLEAGES PASSING
OR GETTING SERIOUSLY INJURED.
IT DOESN'T GET ANY EASIER. NO
MATTER WHAT YOU DO OR THINK
OF ITS ALWAYS IN THE BACK
OF YOUR MIND THAT IT COULD
BE YOU NEXT. SO TO THAT END
I THINK YOU SHOULD NEVER
TAKE LIFE SERIOUSLY, GO OUT
AND TRY NEW THINGS, TRAVEL, HOLD
YOUR FAMILY & FRIENDS CLOSE AND
MAKE EVERY MINUTE COUNT.

LOVE THE LIFE YOU LIVE
LIVE THE LIFE YOU LOVE

OF FRIENDS AND COLLEAGES PASSING
OR GETTING SERIOUSLY INJURED.
IT DOESN'T GET ANY EASIER. NO
MATTER WHAT YOU DO OR THINK
OF ITS ALWAYS IN THE BACK
OF YOUR MIND THAT IT COULD
BE YOU NEXT. SO TO THAT END
I THINK YOU SHOULD NEVER
TAKE LIFE SERIOUSLY, GO OUT
AND TRY NEW THINGS, TRAVEL, HOLD
YOUR FAMILY & FRIENDS CLOSE AND
MAKE EVERY MINUTE COUNT.

LOVE THE LIFE YOU LIVE
LIVE THE LIFE YOU LOVE

We said bye to him and
sent his body home

last night was a very
emotional time, due to the
fact of Davis's body was
sent back home to the uk
and we had a gathering
to see him off. Not everyone
turned up because it was
optional but the hole of 5
plattoon and a few others
turned up. The company
commander Major turner said
fair well and played some
music and we all said
good bye for the last time.
being a father out here at
these Trajic times really makes
you think what you leave back
home. After we said bye to
him and sent his body home
me and the rest of the
Plattoon gave Davis one last
salute.

last night was a very
emotional time, due to the
fact of Davis's body was
sent back home to the uk
and we had a gathering
to see him off. Not everyone
turned up because it was
optional but the hole of 5
plattoon and a few others
turned up. The company
commander Major turner said
fair well and played some
music and we all said
good bye for the last time.
being a father out here at
these Trajic times really makes
you think what you leave back
home. After we said bye to
him and sent his body home
me and the rest of the
plattoon gave Davis one last
salute.

That's enough of my shower time

FOB LIFE IN AFGHAN CAN BE ①
VERY MUNDANE. CLEANING EQUIPMENT,
DOING STAG DUTIES AND FREQUENT
PATROLS.
ON THE OTHER HAND WHERE ELSE COULD
YOU HAVE A SHOWER,
IN A MAKESHIFT SHOWER AREA
WITH NO ROOF WHILE THE SUN IS
BEAMING DOWN ON YOU.
I LOOK UP TO SEE AN APACHE
HELICOPTER FLY OVER HEAD TO SUPPORT
FRIENDLY FORCES NEARBY.
THE EXCHANGE OF GUNFIRE IN THE
DISTANCE WITH AMERICAN A10s
DIVING DOWN IN PLAIN VIEW TAKING
TURNS TO STRAIFE ENEMY POSITIONS.
ALL OF THIS WHILE THE FARMER
ON THE OTHERSIDE OF THE WALL
NEXT TO ME IS HAPPILY DRIVING HIS
TRACTOR GOING ABOUT HIS DAY

AS IF NOTHING IS GOING ON. ②
I CANT HELP BUT THINK,
(AS I SOAP UP)
THESE THINGS WE SEE HERE EVERYDAY
ARE EXTRAORDINARY.
YET WE GET USED TO IT.

WELL THATS ENOUGH ABOUT MY
SHOWER TIME

MORTAR MAN
1ST BN IRISH GUARDS
N° 2 COMPANY
FOB KARNIKAH.

AS IF NOTHING IS GOING ON.
I CAN'T HELP BUT THINK.
(AS I SOAP UP)
THESE THINGS WE SEE HERE EVERYDAY
ARE EXTRAORDINARY.
YET WE GET USED TO IT.

WELL THAT'S ENOUGH ABOUT MY
SHOWER TIME

MORTAR MAN
1ST BN IRISH GUARDS
No2 COMPANY
FOB KARNIKAH

40 letters from children

I have a friend who is a primary
school teacher in the uk. She spoke of
me to her students and with that
I received 40 letters from children of
all ages. They wrote how proud they
were to right to me, that I and my
collegues were doing a great job for
our country. To receive such letters
reinforces my hope that society
in Britain is still proud of it's Forces
and are willing to show them how
proud they are!

I have a friend who is a primary
School teacher in the UK. She spoke of
me to her students and with that
I received two letters from children of
all ages. They wrote how proud they
were to write to me, that I and my
Colleagues were doing a great job for
our country. To receive such letters
reinforces my hope that society
in Britain is still proud of it's Forces
and are willing to show them how
proud they are!

Love on the front line

LOVE ON THE FRONT LINE

MY TOUR WAS GOING WELL and I was
ACTUALLY ENJOYING IT FIGHTING THE TALIBAN
THEN WE GOT A NEW MEDIC. AS I SEEN HER
GET OFF THE CHOPPER AND AS HER EYES FLUTTERED
AT ME I KNEW SHE WAS SPECIAL. THE FIRST TIME
WE SPOKE WE JUST CLICKED RIGHT AWAY THINGS
WERE GOING SO WELL until she went on R+R and
I found out she wasn't COMING BACK. IF
your reading THIS I MISS YOU SO much and I
hope YOU Get IN touch and we can make
A Proper GO OF THINGS AWAY From the eyes
OF THE TALIBAN
                    BIG J.H. A COY 1 R IRISH

LOVE ON THE FRONT LINE

MY TOUR WAS GOING WELL and I WAS ACTUALLY ENJOYING IT FIGHTING THE TALIBAN THEN WE GOT A NEW MEDIC. AS I SEEN HER GET OFF THE CHOPPER AS AS HER EYES FLUTTERED AT ME I KNEW SHE WAS SPECIAL. THE FIRST TIME WE SPOKE WE JUST CLICKED RIGHT AWAY THINGS WERE GOING SO WELL until SHE WENT ON R+R and I found out she wasn't COMING BACK. IF YOUR reading THIS I MISS YOU SO much and I hope YOU GET IN touch and WE CAN make A GOOD GO OF THINGS AWAY From THE eyes OF THE TALIBAN

BIG J.H. ACOX IRLISH.

I don't think I'll be training tonight

SGT

OP MASSIVE
DURING THE TOUR ONE OF MY TRAINING
PARTNERS WAS L/CPL ▪▪▪▪ . HE
LOVES TRAINING, EVEN EATS RIGHT. SOME
MIGHT SAY HIS A BIT OF A PEST.
  ON THE 29TH DEC 10 WE WERE IN
BAISTION WAITING FOR A HELI ASSUALT
INTO DACTRAN. ME AND ▪▪▪▪ HAD
JUST TRAINED SHOULDERS, AND
DECIDED AFTER THE OP WE WOULD
TRAIN LEGS. DUE TO THE FACT WE
WOULD HAVE A COUPLE OF DAYS
AFTER TO RECOVER.
  30TH DEC 10 WE WERE IN DACTRAN
AND A CONTACT HAD STARTED. C33A
HAD BEEN HIT. FOUR CASUALTIES.

SGT

OP MASSIVE

DURING THE TOUR ONE OF MY TRAINING
PARTNERS WAS LCPL ███████. HE
LOVES TRAINING, EVEN EATS RIGHT. SOME
MIGHT SAY HIS A BIT OF A PEST.
  ON THE 29TH DEC 10 WE WERE IN
BIASTION WAITING FOR A HELI ASSUALT
INTO DACTRAN. ME AND ████ HAD
JUST TRAINED SHOULDERS, AND
DECIDED AFTER THE OP WE WOULD
TRAIN LEGS. DUE TO THE FACT WE
WOULD HAVE A COUPLE OF DAYS
AFTER TO RECOVER.
  30TH DEC 10 WE WERE IN DACTRAN
AND A CONTACT HAD STARTED. C33A
HAD BEEN HIT. FOUR CASUALTIES.

L/CPL ■■■■ WAS ONE.

I WAS ONE OF THE FIRST ON THE SCENE. ROUNDS WERE STILL LANDING IN AND AROUND US WHEN I CASEVACED ■■■■ OUT OF THE DANGER AREA ON A PAIR OF LADDERS.

MY MEMORABLE MOMENT WAS JUST BEFORE THIS. I LOOKED DOWN AT ■■■■ ASKING IF HE WAS OK. THE FIRST THING OUT OF HIS MOUTH WAS "GRIFF I DON'T THINK I WILL BE TRAINING LEGS TONIGHT." AT THIS WE GAVE EACH OTHER A LITTLE GRIN.

HE'D BEEN HIT ONCE IN THE LEFT LEG AND THREE TIMES IN THE RIGHT LEG.

LICPL ████████ WAS ONE.

I WAS ONE OF THE FIRST ON THE SCENE. ROUNDS WERE STILL LANDING IN AND AROUND US WHEN I CASEVACED ████████ OUT OF THE DANGER AREA ON A PAIR OF LADDERS.

MY MEMERABLE MOMENT WAS JUST BEFORE THIS. I LOOKED DOWN AT ██████ ASKING IF HE WAS OK. THE FIRST THING OUT OF HIS MOUTH WAS "GRIFF I DON'T THINK I WILL BE TRAINING LEGS TONIGHT." AT THIS WE GAVE EACH OTHER A LITTLE GRIN.

HE'D BEEN HIT ONCE IN THE LEFT LEG. AND THREE TIMES IN THE RIGHT LEG.

Afghanistan needs us

I would like to say
for Afghans to study
& help your country
Afghanistan needs
us.

جريده ملي ښوونکي ادلي عزت زاده   ورته کوو

اردوی ملي افغانستان

نرښا و هر افغان ته دا دنيا ده سلامتيلن

مسکونه زده کړی او د خيل ميواد ديريا

رغونه کی زيار او زحمت ورباسي

او زمو هر افغان نخه د احيله ده چي

د خيل دين او اسلام په مقابل دفاع

وکړي عزت زاده

God's the next man you will meet

Its hard to explain what it
feels like to know one of your
friends have been hit.
Its easy to feel like you will be
hit next.
Its hard to explain the thoughts
in your head after rounds have
landed inches from your feet.
Its easy to think that God's
the next man you will meet.
Men have been to war before us
Its easy to think they were
warriors afraid off nothing but
they were just men like us.
the difference between us and you
is that we will push through fear
for victory is always so near
    Pte, 2 PARA
        D COY

Its hard to explain what it feels like to know one of yours friends have been hit.

Its easy to feel like you will be hit next.

It's hard to explain the thoughts in your head after rounds have landed inches from your feet.

Its easy to think that God's the next man you will meet.

Men have been to war before us

Its easy to think they were warriors afraid of nothing but they were just men like us, the difference between us and you is we will push through fear for victory is always so near

Pte   2 PARA

D COY

My mother's battle with cancer

How family life
back home in Ireland
had influence on me
in afganistan

Ranger Curley
     1 Royal Irish

Pg 1

How family life
back home in Ireland
had influence on me
in afganiston

Rangee Curley
     1 Royal Irish

Its my 1st time here and has been an experience, alot of mixed feelings and scary moments but some how under all this poverty and wartorn country I still find connections to home in ways by seen children playing games just like I did but without the soilders and the threat of Taliban on their families.

The one major comparison I have is we had a contact one day in which the Taliban ambush us and we pinned down taking fire from 3

Pg 2

ts my 1st time here and has been an experience, alot of mixed feelings and scary moments but some how under all this poverity and wartorn country I still find connections to home in ways by seen children playing games just like I did but without the soilders and and the threat of Taliban on their families.

the one major comparsion I have is we had a contact one day in which The Taliban ambushe us and we pinned down taking fire from 3

positions we had no choice but
to make a sprint across open ground
cause we could not use the ditch
cause of the IED threat. Once we
took off across the open ground they
started to smash us, it was crazy
round going everywhere. It was not a
case of am I going to get shot it was
where am i going to get shot. With
the help of God and the drive of a
soilder we all made it across. We
patrolled back when it died down but
as we walked back to the base i seen
what looked like a father and son
working in the fields. It brought
my mind back

Pg3

positions we had no choice but
to make a sprint across open ground
cause we could not use the ditch
cause of the IED threat. Once we
took off across the open ground they
started to smash us, it was crazy
round going everywhere. It was not a
care of am i going to get shot it was
where am i going to get shot. With
the help of God and the drive of a
soilder we all made it across. We
patrolled back when it died down but
as we walked back to the base i seen
what looked like a father and son
working in the fields. It brought
my mind back

to when me and my father worked
together making a living for our family
but the only battle we had was
the one my mother had to fight off
cancer and the only soilder we had in our
safe environment in the west of
Ireland was my mam cause she
fought and still fights her illness
                              What
i am trying to say is no matter where
you go in life or what you do your
family memories will never be forgotten
and influence you many ways
without you even known.
                    If any younger
children read this all i can say

Pg 5

is treasure your family cause thinking about them can get you through the toughest times in life even if its the hell hole of the earth like helmand afganistan

Ranger Curley
1 Royal Irish

is treasure your family cause
thinking about them can get
you through the toughest
times in life even if it's the
hell hole of the earth like
helmand afganistan

Ranger Curley
1 Royal Irish

Stretchers against the wall

STRETCHERS AGAINST THE WALL

THEY STAND AGAINST THE HOSPITAL WALL
LIKE SOLDIERS STOOD Parade Ground tall
THEY CARRY THE INJURED, The Brave & fallen
To an OASIS STAFED by those CALLEN
THE IMPRINT FOREVER DUSTY & STARK
LEAVES IT OWN lasting mark
OF LIFES EBB & FLOW THIS DAY
OF a SOLDIERS LIFE PASSING BY THIS WAY

PADRE
Engineers & Counter IED

STRETCHERS AGAINST THE WALL

THEY STAND AGAINST THE HOSPITAL WALL
LIKE SOLDIERS STOOD PARADE GROUND TALL
THEY CARRY THE INJURED, THE BRAVE & FALLEN
TO AN OASIS STAFFED BY THOSE CALLED
THE IMPRINT FOREVER DUSTY & STARK
LEAVES IT ONLY lasting mark
OF LIFES EBB & FLOW THIS DAY
OF A SOLDIERS LIFE PASSING BY THIS WAY

Padre
Engineer & Counter IED

Nothing compares to the first time getting shot at

HERRICK 13 2010

Nothing compares to the first time getting
shot at. Adrenaline is sky high and
lasts ages. But saying that I think the
first time I saw one of the lads getting
injured was probably one of the
worst things i have ever had to deal
with.

HERRICK 13 2010

Nothing compares to the first time getting shot at. Adrenaline is sky high and lasts ages. But saying that, i think the first time i saw one of the lads getting injured was probably one of the worst things i have ever had to deal with.

Long days and nights, even longer days

RGR DALZELL from Bangor N. Ireland

What can i say Afghan eh. This is my first tour and it's been tough lyk. there has been long day's and night's, even longer day's. At the start when we first got here you couldnt even leave the CP without getn shot at. The start was very good tho never a dull day. I'm a UGL gunner so it's even more fun when we get a contact.

I'm gonna finish by saying 1 word and only 1 work.
"STAG"

RGR DALZELL from Bangor N Ireland

What can I say Afgoon eh. This
is my first tour and it's been
tough lyk, there has been long
days and night's, even longer
days, At the start when we
first got here you couldn't even
leave the CP without getin shot
at. the start was very good
tho never a dull day. I'm a
UGL gunner so it's even more
fun when we get a contact.
I'm gonna finish by saying
I word and only 1 work.
           "STAG"

Go and leave them in peace

I HAVE WORKED HARD WITH ISAF AND NOW WE HAVE A VERY GOOD RELATIONSHIP WITH ALL THE LOCALS. NOW THE TALIBAN TRY THEIR HARDEST TO DESTROY THIS RELATIONSHIP, BECAUSE THEY HAVE LOST THEIR CONTROL OF THE LOCAL, AND ARE ANGRY BECAUSE THE LOCALS WISH THEM TO GO AND LEAVE THEM IN PEACE.
SAID
KABUL
AFGHANISTAN.
JAN 2011.

I HAVE WORKED HARD WITH ISAF AND NOW WE HAVE A VERY GOOD RELATIONSHIP WITH ALL THE LOCALS. NOW THE TALIBAN TRY THEIR HARDEST TO DESTROY THIS RELATIONSHIP, BECAUSE THEY HAVE LOST THEIR CONTROL OF THE LOCALS, AND ARE ANGRY BECAUSE THE LOCALS WISH THEM TO GO AND LEAVE THEM IN PEACE.

Said

Kabul

Afghanistan.

Jan 2011.

Parcels from home

Just back from a 5 hour patrol
Recieved parcels on 21/01/2011
17:51 afghan time

Tortilla wraps
caned chicken
caned Ham
coffee (Nescafe not issued) taste the
                                difference
Gloves
cookies
sweets
its such moral it's unbelievable

Just back from a 5 hour patrol
Recieved parcels on 21/01/2011
17:51 afghan time

Tortilla wraps
Coned chicken
Coned Ham
Coffee (Nescofe not issued) taste the
difference
Gloves
Cockies
Sweets
its such moral it's unbelivable

The Medical Officer's conundrum

XXX.I.MMXI

THE MEDICAL OFFICER'S CONUNDRUM:

"PROVIDED ALL GOES WELL AND ACCORDING TO PLAN THEN THE DOCTOR IS DESTINED TO BE BORED…"

THE YOUNG SOLDIER WAS BROUGHT TO ME FOLLOWING AN IED BLAST. HIS INJURIES WERE SERIOUS THOUGH THE MEDIC IN HIS PATROL HAD ALREADY SAVED HIS LIFE. ALL I COULD ADD TO THIS WAS A REASSESSMENT OF HIS INJURIES AND AN OFFER OF STRONGER ANALGESIA. HE DECLINED THE LATTER AND LAY IN SILENCE ON THE STRETCHER AMONGST THE DUST.
        I DIDN'T NEED TO ASK MANY MORE QUESTIONS – HIS EYES TOLD THE WHOLE STORY. AS WIDE AS POSSIBLE AND CONVEYING SUCH A SENSE OF BEWILDERMENT, UNCERTAINTY AND TERROR THAT I SHALL NEVER FOREGT THEM.

CAPT,
MEDICAL OFFICER
D COY 2 PARA

THE MEDICAL OFFICER'S CONUNDRUM:

"PROVIDED ALL GOES WELL AND ACCORDING TO PLAN THEN THE DOCTOR IS DESTINED TO BE BORED..."

_____

THE YOUNG SOLDIER WAS BROUGHT TO ME FOLLOWING AN IED BLAST. HIS INJURIES WERE SERIOUS THOUGH THE MEDIC IN HIS PATROL HAD ALREADY SAVED HIS LIFE. ALL I COULD ADD TO THIS WAS A REASSESSMENT OF HIS INJURIES AND AN OFFER OF STRONGER ANALGESIA. HE DECLINED THE LATTER AND LAY IN SILENCE ON THE STRETCHER AMONGST THE DUST.

I DIDN'T NEED TO ASK MANY MORE QUESTIONS - HIS EYES TOLD THE WHOLE STORY - AS WIDE AS POSSIBLE AND CONVEYING SUCH A SENSE OF BEWILDERMENT, UNCERTAINTY AND TERROR THAT I SHALL NEVER FORGET THEM.

CAPT
MEDICAL OFFICER
D COY 2 PARA.

Not fixing bayonets

CPL GAV MARTIN 1 ROYAL IRISH
CP MANGOOL

THE HARDEST THING FOR
ME WAS NOT FIXING
BAYONET'S
BUT LEAVING MY SON
WHO I ONLY GOT TO
SEE FOR 1 WEEK

CPL GAV MARTIN 1 ROYAL IRISH
CP MANGOOL

THE HARDEST THING FOR
ME WAS NOT FIXING
BAYONET'S
BUT LEAVING MY SON
WHO I ONLY GOT TO
SEE FOR 1 WEEK

Death Alley

Clearing an AFGHAN VILLAGE
called CHAR-COCHA in HELMAND,
OF IEDSs. Locals are under-
standing the Good were
doing by making their village
safe. I know by first
hand How devastating a IED
AS I Got hit Down a Place
called 'Death Alley'. Got
shrapnel to the leg but my
mates got hit worse. ■■■■
had his kneecap blown off &
■■■■ had his shoulder smashed.
The bang and having ■■■■
blood over me when fixing him
up will always stay with
me. So its satisfying to
see the same area being made
safe and our work being
appreciated !

Pte MAXFIELD

Clearing an AFGHAN VILLAGE
called CHAR-COCHA in HELMAND,
OF IEDs. Locals are under-
standing the Good were
doing by making their village
safe. i know by first
hand How devistating a IED
AS I Got hit Down a Place
called 'Death Alley'. Got
sharpnel to the leg but my
Mates got hit worse. ████
had his kneecap blown off &
████ had his shoulder smashed.
The bang and having ████ him
blood over me when fixing him
up will always stay with
me. so its satisfying to
see the some area being made
safe and our work being
appreciated! PTE MAXFIELD

Dream as if you will live forever

Dream as is you Will Live
FOREVER,

Live as is you will die
TommoRRow

Nade Ali, Helmand, Cp Ranger 2011

CP MANGOOL   20/01/11

A COY

Do I miss home well of course
wouldnt you when everyday life
to us in the u.k will now be
classed as a luxury.

My feelings on locals how can they
be helped when they will not help us
help them.

Do I get paid enough hell no
some lolly pop guy or women gets
more for stoping cars than we do for stoping
Sucide Vechiles.

Army chiefs worry more about
what there getting paid and trying to
impress other officers than the welfare
and Suffery of Soldiers on the ground

Will I still have a girlfriend?

CP MANGOOL   20/01/11

A COY

Do I miss home well of course
wouldnt you when everyday life
to us in the u.k will now be
classed as a luxury.

My feelings on locals how can they
be helped when they will not help us
help them.

Do I get paid enough hell no
some lolly pop guy or woman gets
more for stoping cars then we do for stoping
sucide vechiles.

Army chiefs worry more about
what there getting paid and trying to
impress other officers than the welfare
and suffering of soldiers on the ground

A COY

We as soldiers have a completely differnt way of thinking about this war Civiys think It must be awful perants dont sleep with worry, my boy is out there getting shot at ha well thats what we love getting shot at is nothing It feels amazing until you get the come down then you realise how lucky u've been, so you see it's not the bullets that scare us its the I.E.D's how would you feel if you lost your leg. I dont feel Id be accepted could I really have the same life would my girlfriend even stay with me.

CP MANGOOL   20/01/2011

A COY

We as Soldiers have a completeing differnt way of thinking about this war Civiys think It must be awful perants dont sleep with worry, my boy is out there getting shot at ha well thats what we love getting shot at is nothing It feels amazing until you get the come down then you realise how lucky u've been, So you see it's not the bullets that scare us its the I.E.D's how would you feel if you lost your leg. I dont feel Id be accepted could I really have the Same life would my girlfriend even stay with me.

CP MANGOOL   20/01/11

A COY

8 weeks to go and yes I am counting
not just in weeks but days to
every night I stand on stag in the
freezing cold making sure we keep camp
secure I think fuck it not long
to go, paranoia going through your
head have things changed at home will
I still have a girlfriend, how will people
see me now or should I even
care this is me this is what I do
I'm helping this country why cant
the viewers at home see my quote
            I Shall Not Judge What I Can Not See!

CP MANGod   20/01/2011

A coy

8 weeks to go and yes I am counting
not just in weeks but days to
every night I stand on stag in the
freezing cold making sure we keep camp
secure I think fuck it not long
to go, paranoia going through your
head have things changed at home will
I still have a girlfriend, how will people
see me now or should I even
care this is me this is what I do
I'm helping this country why cant
the viewers at home see my quote

  I Shall NOT Judge what I can Not See!

109

My gorgeous girl

PTE, 23 Pioneer

I am 20 years old and been
in the army for 2 ½ years now.
This is my first operational Tour
and since we have been in
Theater we've had our up's and
down's but as a Team we have
stuck together and got through it
all. When I arived in Afghanistan
I was very sceptical of Doing a tour
as a Searcher in part of the C-IED
Taskforce but after we got out on the
ground and Done a few task's
it got easier an easier, Day by Day.
We are now 4 weeks away from
R and R and really looking
forward to getting home to see
friend and family and of course
My gorgeous girl Lucie.

PTE, 23 PioneeR

I am 20 years old and been in the army for 2½ years now. This is my first operational tour and since we have been in Theater we've had our ups and down's but as a Team we have stuck together and got through it all. When I arived in Afghinistan I was very Sceptical of Doing a tour as a Searcher in Part of the C-IED Taskforce but after we got out on the ground and Done a few task's it got easier and easier, Day by Day. We are now 4 weeks away from R and R and really Looking sorword to getting home to see friend and family and of course My gorgeous girl Lucie.

They are like ghosts

When I went home on R+R people asked me have you ever seen the taliban and I told them I have been fired at loads of times but only ever seen 1 taliban with a weapon they are like goasts.

When I went home on R+R
People asked me have you ever
Seen the taliban and I told
them I have been fired at
loads of times but only ever
seen 1 taliban with a weapon
they are like goasts.

Health and Safety rules

FOB KNK JAN 2011

Who lets these 'BASTION CAMP Rats' come out of their holes
to the Real World to lecture the FORWARD OPERATING BASE
(Its all in the title) about Health + Safety ???
All I Get Is a Pompous Self Important 'Leaf Eater' asking
where is YOUR SIGN for this? Where is YOUR SIGN for that?
Why have you not got a sign saying FIRE EXTINGUISHER above
the FIRE EXTINGUISHER that's painted bright red with FIRE
EXTINGUISHER written in Bold white writing on it?? Why
have your Sangers not got a hand rail on the steps up.
If they ever were to visit Planet Earth I would inform
them that in a Sanger having no hand rail is the
least of your worries…..I would suggest the 7.62mm

Short or the RPG winging its way Towards You Is of a Bigger Concern!! And Signs for Hazards!!! I wood Really like Someone to visit the Taliban and tell them to Pot Signs on their Pressure Plate IED's as I am finding them to be a Real Hazard!! To All Health and Safety Guru's Drawing the Queens Shilling. *PLEASE* Stay In Bastion with all the Other 'Leaf Eaters' and Stay the f*@k out of my FOB or I may Just take You Out with Us 'Meat Eaters' on a Patrol In the 'Green Zone' and then You will See Some Health + Safety ISSUES!!

Quis Separabit

short or the RPG winging its way towards you is
of a BIGGER Concern!! AND SIGNS for HAZARDS!!!
I would Really like someone to visit the Taliban
and tell them to Put SIGNS on their Pressure Plate
IED's as I am finding them to be a Real Hazard!!
To All Health and Safety Guru's Drawing the Queens
Shilling. PLEASE stay in Bastion with all the other
'Leaf Eaters' and stay the f*@k out of my FOB or
I may just take you out with us 'Meat Eaters' on
a Patrol in the 'GREEN ZONE' and then you will
see some Health and Safety ISSUES!!
QUIS SEPARABIT

The unsung heroes

People back home hear
about the deaths out
here but they dont
hear about the injurys
soldiers get or hear
about the unsung heros
the medical team in
bastion who do a
job second two none

People back home hear about the deaths out here but they dont hear about the injurys soldiers get or hear about the unsung heros the medical team in bastion who do a job second two none

A real chance of life

Well it's my first tour, it's been hard but also rewarding. Seeing the massive change to the Community and bonding with all the lads. Im not gonna write about another contact, just let you all know its not all fighting it's also about giving the people of AFGHANISTAN a real chance at life.

RGR,

Spectamur Agendo

Well it's my first tour, It's been hard but also rewarding. Seeing the massive change to the Community and bonding with all the lads. Im not gonna write about another Contact, Just let you all Know its not all Fighting it's also about giving the people of AFGHANISTAN a real chance at life.

      RGR

         Spectamur Agendo

Like I had just survived a really bad car crash

Just a Normal Day Just a Normal
Patrol IN The after noon IN AFGanStan
I had Been on a patrol For around
2 Hour's when we got Contacted.
By Pkm Fire. This was Normal
we usely got contacted every Day
So The Section I was with Jumped
IN To A 6 Feet Deep Ditch Soon
the Fire stopet then we moved in to
a more Shallower ERagesion Ditch
around 4 Feet Deep Filled with
Water. and Carryed on Patrolling.

Just a Normal Day Just a Normal
Patrol In The after Noon IN AFGanstan
I had Been on a patrol For around
2 Hour's when we got contacted
By Pkm Fire. This was Normal
we usely got contacted every Day.
So the section I was with Jumped
IN To A 6 Feet Deep Ditch Soon
the Fire stopet then we moved in to
a more shallower Eragesion Ditch
around 4 Feet Deep Filled with
water and carryed on patrolling.

When a Second Burst of machine
Gun Fire started At the same
Time a shot Landed about
2 meter's in Front of me. This is
what Tailban sniper's Do they Aim
At your Feet then Bring there Aim
up. The second shot Hit my
Helmet on The Lucky Shamrock the
Force knocked me off my Feet AND
I was smurged in the water For
How Long I Don't know I was kind
off knocked out For a Few second's
The next thing I remember was a Bang
and a Flash where the

When a Second Burst oF machine
Gun Fire Started At the same
Time a ~~shot~~ shot Landed aBout
2 meter's iN Front oF me, This iS
what TailBan sniPer'S Do They Aim
AT your Feet then Bring there Aim
up. The Second Shot Hit my
Helmet oN The Lucky ShamRock the
Force knocked me oFF my Feet AND
I was Smurged in the water For
How Long I Dont know I was kind
oFF knocked out For a Few Second'S
The nexT thing I RemenBer was a Bang
and a Flash where the

Ranger Be side me Fired a "bb" which is kinda lyk a Rocket Luncher. I got my self up out of the water seen where the enemy was and Fired until I Ran out of Round's changed my mag Then checked For Blood At First I thought I was shot In the Face But When I couldnt Find any Blood I Just kept on Fireing until The enemy stopt. I was still veary Confused about wat happend. only When I got Back

Ranger Be side me Fired a "bb"
which is kinda lyk a Rocket Luncher.
I got my self up out of the
water seen where the enemy
was and Fired until I Ran
out of Round's changed my mag
Then checked For Blood At First
I thought I was shot In the
Face But when I couldnt Find any
Blood I Just kept on Fireing until
The enemy stopt. I was still veary
confused about wat happened. only
when I got Back

IN To my check point and
was able to take my Body Armor
And Helmet off my section command
came up to me to make sure I was ok
And put His Finger threw the Hole
where the Bullet Had actuly Just
gone threw my Helmet cover.
I felt extremely Lucky Like I
Had Just survied a Really bad car crash.

A Lucky
RANGER From
Northern Ireland.

IN To my check point and
was able to take my BoDy ARmor
And Helmet off my section command
came up to me to make sure I was ok
And put His Finger threw the Hore
where the Bullet Had actuly Just
gone threw my Helmet cover.
I Felt extremly Lucky Like I
Had Just survied a Really Bad cer crash.

A Lucky
RANGER From
Nolthern EReland

Sometimes the clock stops

Sometimes i'd rather be
nowhere else.
Sometime i'd rather be
anywhere else.
Sometimes it feels like home.
Sometimes home feels a long
way from here.
Sometimes time flies.
Sometimes the clock stops.
Sometimes we have to withdraw.
Sometimes we take the fight
to them.

Always we're in it
together.

Sometimes i'd rather be nowhere else

Sometimes i'd rather be anywhere else

Sometimes it feels like home.
Sometimes home feels a long way from here.

Sometimes time flies.
Sometimes the clock stops.

Sometimes we have to withdraw.
Sometimes we take the fight to them.

Always we're in it together

Public duties

GDSM GOVAN 30110703 IRISH GUARDS
Cant wait to get back from this tour
and do some public duties!!!!!!
Back to the joy's of streetlining or
Queen's guard's.
Should have brought the drill boot's with
me and layered them up everynight would
be gleaming by the time I'm back HA.

GDSM GOVAN 30110703 IRISH GUARDS.

Cant wait to get back from this tour
and do some public duties!.!!!!
Back to the joys of streetlining or
Queen's guard's.
Should have brought the drill boot's with
me and layered them up everynight would
be gleaming by the time I'm back HA.

Grenades

Gone firm behind a
wall and see 2 grenades
flying towards us.

Being bored a lot of the
time and looking forward
to R+R in 4 days.

Clearing the village of ied's
and having people move
back has been really good
to be a part and making it
safe for the locals again.

Gone firm behind a
wall and see 2 grenades
flying towards us.

Being bored a lot of the
time and looking forward
to R+R in 4 days.

Clearing the village of ied's
and having people move
back has been really good
to be a part and making it
safe for the locals again.

Dust

MY ABIDING MEMORY OF AFGHANISTAN?
More like DUSTISTAN! The dust, it gets everywhere!
Its not:

- Playing football with a squeeling bunch of ANA.
- Local kid's faces lighting up at the sight of a pen.
- The crystal clear night skies
- Chef's steak nights
- Making paper-maché heads
- Rugby on the HLS and the OC taking a tumble.

No, it will be a humble local farmer, who one day took
me by surprise by asking after my family. "You are far
from home. You must miss your family very much. We
are very grateful."

DOC RICHARDS

MY ABIDING MEMORY OF AFGHANISTAN?
More like DUSTISTAN! The dust, it gets everywhere!
Its not:
- Playing football with a squeeling bunch of ANA.
- Local kid's faces lighting up at the sight of a pen.
- The crystal clear night skies
- Chef's Steak nights
- Making paper mache heads
- Rugby on the HLS and the OC taking a tumble.
No, it will be a humble local farmer, who one day took
me by suprise by asking after my family. "You are far
from home. You must miss your family very much. We
are very grateful."

DOC RICHARDS

One of the bravest men I've ever met has just lost his legs

IT'S A GREY MISERABLE DAY. WE'VE
BEEN UP SINCE BEFORE SUNRISE. THE
CLOUDS ARE LOW AND HEAVY. RAIN IS
FALLING. THE MUD IS ANKLE DEEP
AND EXHAUSTING. ONE OF THE BRAVEST
MEN I'VE EVER MET HAS JUST LOST HIS LEGS.
HE HAD LED, PAVING THE WAY WITH
HIS METAL DETECTOR. AND HIS REWARD
FOR SUCH COURAGE AND SELFLESSNESS
IS TO BE GREVIOUSLY INJURED. AS YOU
READ THIS BACK IN THE UK, PLEASE, BY
ALL MEANS REMEMBER THE DEAD, BUT
SPARE THOUGHTS FOR MEN SUCH AS
THESE, AND THEIR BROKEN BODIES. THEY
DESERVE THEIR COUNTRY'S LOVE. I HOPE YOU
ADJUST TO YOUR NEW LIFE■■■■ AND
GROWN OLD + FAT + HAPPY! REST EASY +
TAKE SATISFACTION – YOU'VE DONE YOUR BIT!
AND HOW!!

MEDIC

It's a grey miserable day. We've been up since before sunrise. The clouds are low and heavy. Rain is falling. The mud is ankle deep and exhausting. One of the bravest men I've met has just lost his legs. He had led, paving the way with his metal detector. And his reward for such courage and selflessness is to be grievously injured. As you read this back in the UK, please, by all means remember the dead, but spare thoughts for men such as these, and their broken bodies. They deserve their country's love. I hope you adjust to your new life ████████ and grow old + fat + happy! Rest easy + take satisfaction – you've done your bit! And how!!

MKDK

Thanks

I
ISAF and ANA ~~are~~ work
together. They do patrol
day and night for developme
nt
of Afghanistan. ISAF and
ANA sucrifies their
lives for the local people
to bring security. They
work hard twenty four hours
to smash the Taliban and

I
ISAF and ANA work
together. They do patrol
day and night for development
of Afghanistan. ISAF and
ANA sacrifices their
lives for the local people
to bring security. They
work hard twenty four hours
to smash the Taliban and

(2)
Al-quaida. ISAF and
ANA have a great plan
for development and
security. They want to
build hospitals, schools and
clinic for each village.
ANA feel happy to work
with their ISAF friends.

(2)
Al-quaida. ISAF and
ANA have a great plan
for development and
security. They want to
build hospitals, schools and
clinic for each village.
ANA feel happy to work
with their ISAF friends.

(3)
ISAF and ANA will not allow the enimies to destroy again this land. They are far from their families to serve the Army job. Finaly I'm greatful of ISAF to help us in every case.

Thanks
ANA soldiers

ISAF and ANA (3) will not allow the enimies to destroy again this land. They are far from their families to serve the Army Jole. Finaly I'm greatful of ISAF to help us in every case.

Thanks
ANA soldiers

Blood brothers

Tour – Afghanistan 2010 Herrick 13
1R IRISH 16.A.A. Sabat

I was born in New Zealand in Auckland. I came here about end of 2006 then join the British Army to fight The Taliban so are world is safe from terrorism. We fight for each other back to back blood brother's. What we do that's who we are.

Went on Patrol setting off from Sabat to go to compound 13,14 We moved off to go cross country moving in diches and tracks when we was moving back we got contacted from the East and West. from Sabat setting off we went north west then coming back getting contacted ever where North East and Southwest and East then the West.

RGR
SIGNAL

Tour - Afghanistan 2010 Herrick 13
2R   IRISH 16.A.A. Sobat

①

I was born in New Zealand in Auckland. I came here about end of 2006 then Join the British Army to fight The taliban so ove world is Safe from terrorism. ~~Its dont fight for~~ ~~ove country but~~ fight for each other back to back blood brothers. What we do that is who we are.

Went on Patrol Setting off from Sobat to go to compound 13,19 We moved off to go cross country moving in diches and tracks When we was moving back we got Contacted from the East and West. from Sobat Setting off we went noth went then coming back getting ~~contacted~~ contacted every where Noth East and South went and East then the went. RGR
                    SIGNAL

From the trenches to the present

Every time I leave the CP on patrol I pray for a CONTACT.
There is nothing better than getting the rounds down and taking
the fight to the Taliban, getting even for every soldier
injured and killed in this unfixable/unhelpable country.
Im going through what many Infantry soldiers have before
from the trenche's to the present. I love what I do its an
honour to fight for Britain. We fight for each other.

Acoy 1 Royal Irish   RGR T (Rep of Ireland) Faugh-A-Ballagh

Every time I leave the CP on patrol I pray for a CONTACT.

There is nothing better than getting the rounds down and taking the fight to the Taliban; getting even for every soldier injured and killed in this unfixable/unhelpable country.

Im going through what many Infantry soldiers have before from the trenche's to the present. I love what I do its an honour to fight for Britain. We fight for eachother.

Acoy 1 Royal Irish RGR T (Rep of Ireland) Faugh -A- Ballagh

I am happy to sacrifice

A Soldier, I hate
Stag even back in Uk
I don't like being on guard
but out here, it's something
everyone has to do as we
are short of personnel and
every extra bloke counts and
means an extra hour of sleep,
I am happy to sacrifice my
comfort just to help the lads
get through this tour.
I miss my family, my 1 year
2 months old daughter "Christie".
Life is hard being here with a
family back home, especially when
you are getting shot at and you
know anything can happen.
I can't wait to get back home
see my wife, and daughter.

As Soldier, I hate
Stag even back in UK
I don't like being on guard
but Out here, it's something
everyone has to do. as we
are short of personnel and
every extra bloke Counts and
means an extra hour of sleep,
I am happy to sacrifice my
Comfort just to help the lads
get through this tour.

I miss my family, my 1 year
2 months old daughter "Christie".
Life is hard being here with a
family back home, especially when
you are getting shot at and you
know anything can happen.
I can't wait to get back home
see my wife, and daughter.

Have I just seen the man who will kill me?

AVERAGE MEDIC   H13

YOU SEE A LOCAL NATIONAL. ELDERLY.
A NOMAD. HE COMPLAINS HE IS WEAK
AND CANNOT HAVE SEX WITH HIS WIFE.
HE INSISTS ON TABLETS. YOU TELL HIM
HE IS 70 AND THIS IS NORMAL. YOU ARGUE
WITH HIM UNTIL HE GIVES UP.

YOU'RE ON PATROL. AN EAR SPLITTING
EXPLOSION 20 METRES AWAY. A GUARDSMAN
HAS SET OFF AN IED. YOU RUN OVER
TO HIM, YOU SEE HIS LEGS GONE, HIS
ARM HANGING BY SINEW, HIS RIFLE
SMASHED. HE'S DYING. YOUR IN LINE OF
SIGHT OF A TALIBAN POSITION. YOU'RE THE
MEDIC, YOU'RE APPALLED BY THE SIGHT.
CAN YOU SAVE HIM?

IN A CORDON. A MAN JUMPS BEHIND A
MURDER HOLE RIGHT TO YOUR FRONT. 100 METRES
YOU THINK 'HAVE I JUST SEEN THE MAN
WHO WILL KILL ME?'. YOU SHOOT FOR YOUR LIFE

AVERAGE MEDIC H13

You See A Local National. Elderly. A Nomad. He Complains He Is Weak And Cannot Have Sex With His Wife. He Insists On Tablets. You Tell Him He Is 70 And This Is Normal. You Argue With Him Until He Gives Up.

You're On Patrol. An Ear Splitting Explosion 20 metres Away. A Guardsman Has Set Off An IED. You Run Over To Him, You See His Legs Gone, His Arm Hanging By Skin, His Rifle Smashed. He's Dying. You In Line Of Sight Of A Taliban Position. You're The Medic, You're Paralysed By The Sight. Can You Save Him?

In A Cordon. A Man Jumps Behind A Murder Hole Right To Your Front. 100 metres You Think 'Have I Just Seen The Man Who Will Kill Me?'. You Shoot For Your Life

The only ones to understand will have stood where we now stand

PB KALANG   CFNDA(S)   SAIDABAD

Deploying out here certainly makes you appreciate the gifts you have in life. You wish for the small things from home. Taking things just 1 day at a time. The Tasks that these soldiers perform on a daily basis are remarkable. They are not here for politics or to try & put the worlds problems to rest. When you are heavily engaged & the dirt is lifting at your feet. You are here for the people left & right of you & to ensure that you do the right thing. It will be hard to try & explain to people exactly what its like. That's why the only ones to understand will have stood where we now stand. The excitement in contact & the coming down after & silent reflection. Its just another day in Saidabad.
Faugh-a-Ballagh -
A COY 1 R IRISH.

PB KALANG CF NDA (S)   SAIDABAD

Deploying out here certainly makes you
appreciate the gifts you have in life. You
wish for the small things from home.
Taking things just 1 day at a time. The
tasks that these soldiers perform on a daily
basis are remarkable. They are not here for
politics or to try + put the worlds problems
to rest. When you are heavily engaged +
the dirt is lifting at your feet. You are
here for the people left + right of you
+ to ensure that you do the right
thing. It will be hard to try + explain to
people exactly what its like. Thats why the
only ones to understand will have stood where
we now stand. The excitement in contact +
the coming down after + silent reflection. Its
just another day in Saidabad.

        Faugh - a - Ballagh -

A COY 1 R IRISH.

My medical centre is a shipping container

I am a combat medical technician.
My regiment is 16 medical Regiment.
My medical centre is an iso container.
This container is capable of a lot more than just storage
My ambulance is my bergan with a stretcher straped to its side
My welcome to Afghanistan was a massive explosion
The place is strange
Make the most of what you have
Do the most for the most
That's indeed is how we roll.

Attendance and Treatment Card

Card Serial No.

(Service No.)	(Rank/Rating (pencil)	(Christian or Forename(s))	(Surname)	Branch Trade

Date	Place where treated	Short notes showing Complaints, Symptoms, Diagnosis, Treatment, etc.	Disposal	M.O.'s signature

I am a combat medical technician
My regiment is 16 medical Regiment
My medical centre is an iso container
This container is capable of a lot more than just storage
My ambulance is my bergan with a stretcher strapped to its side
My welcome to Afghanistan was a massive explosion
The place is strange
Make the most of what you have
Do the most for the most
That's indeed is how we roll

CMT

149

A fact I credit to Jesus and Jesus alone

MY NAMES IS JAMES JONES, A AM A SGT OF
THE UNTED STATES MARINE CORP, I SERVE AS A FIRE SUPPORT MAN
IN A SPECIALIZED TEAM OF FIRE SUPPORT SPECIALIST.
IN WINTER 2010 – SUMMER 2011 WE WERE
ATTACHED TO A US ARMY SF TEAM IN ORDER
TO PROVIDE THEM QUALIFYIED OBSERVERS FOR CLOSE
AIR SUPPORT AND MOTAR'S AS THEY CONDUCTED
VILLAGE STABILITY OPERATIONS IN THE AREA
OF MIRMINDAB. THIS IS MY SECOND TOUR IN AFGHANISTAN
AND THE FOLLOWING STORY IS MY ACCOUNT OF THE FIRST
OF MANY ENGAGEMENTS W/ THE ENEMY
DURING THIS TOUR OUR OBJ WAS TO TAKE OVER
A COMPOUND NORTH OF OUR MAIN BASE FOR IT'S
STRATEGIC ADVANTAGE OF CONTROLING A NEARBY
BRIDGE, A MAIN SUPPY ROUTE FOR

MY NAME IS James ~~████████~~ JONES, A AM A SGT OF
THE UNITED STATES MARINE CORP, I SERVE AS A FIRE SUPPORT MAN
IN A SPECIALIZED TEAM OF FIRE SUPPORT SPECIALIST.
IN ~~2010~~ WINTER 2010 - SUMMER 2011 WE ~~WE~~ WERE
ATTACHED TO A US ARMY SF TEAM ~~TO PP~~ IN ORDER
TO PROVIDE THEM QUALIFYIED OBSERVERS FOR CLOSE
AIR SUPPORT AND MOTAR'S AS THEY CONDULTED

VILLAGE STABILITY OPERATIONS IN THE ~~AR~~ AREA
OF MIRMINDAB. THIS IS MY SECOND TOUR IN AFRGANISTA
AND THE FOLLOWING STORY IS MY ACCOUNT OF THE FIRST
OF MANY ENGAGEMENTS W/ THE ENEMY ~~FOR THIS~~
DURING THIS TOUR. OUR OBJ WAS TO TAKE OVER
A COMPOUND NORTH OF OUR MAIN BASE FOR IT'S
STRATEGIC ADVANTAGE OF CONTROLING A NEARBY
BRIDGE, A MAIN ~~ROUTE OF AOV~~ SUPPY ROUTE FOR

INSURGENCE. WE HAD SUCCESSFULLY
CAPTURED THE COMPOUND AND ESTABLISHED 360°
SECURITY. I WAS JUST RELIEVED OF THE NE
SECURITY POSITION AND WAS LOOKING FOR ANY BASE
IMPROVEMENT TASK I COULD ASSIST IN WHEN WE
BEGAN TO RECEIVE EFFECTIVE AK.47 FIRE FROM
A COMPOUND 300 METERS TO THE WEST
ON THE OTHER SIDE OF A CANAL. WHILE OUR WESTERN
SECURITY POST ENGAGED W/ HEAVY MACHINE GUN FIRE
MYSELF, 4 US ARMY SF, AND ABOUT 5 ANA SF RUSHED
TO THE WESTERN WALL TO SUPPRESS THE ENEMY
W/ SMALL ARMS FIRE WHILE CLOSE AIR SUPPORT WAS
CALLED.
SOON THE ENEMY WAS OVERWHELMED AND PINNED
DOWN. THROUGH A COMBINATION OF GUN RUNS AND A 500lB BOMB
THE ENEMY WAS DESTROYED. WE EXPERIENCED NO
CAUSUALTIES THAT DAY, A FACT I CREDIT TO JESUS AND JESUS
ALONE.

INSURGENCE. WE HAD SUCCESSFULLY ~~COMMANDER~~ CAPTURED THE COMPOUND AND ESTABLISHED 360° SECURITY. ~~WH~~ I ~~was~~ WAS JUST RELIEVED OF THE NE SECURITY POSITION AND WAS LOOKING FOR ANY BASE IMPROVEMENT TASK I COULD ASSIST IN WHEN WE BEGAN TO RECIEVE EFFECTIVE AK-47 FIRE FROM ~~THE WE TO~~ A COMPOUND 300 METERS TO THE WEST ON THE OTHER SIDE OF A CANAL. WHILE OUR WESTERN SECURITY POST ENGAGED w/ HEAVY MACHINE GUN FIRE MYSELF, 4 US ARMY SF, AND ~~ABOUT~~ 5 ANA SF RUSHED TO THE WESTERN WALL TO SUPPRESS THE ENEMY w/ SMALL ARMS FIRE WHILE CLOSE AIR SUPPORT WAS CALLED. ~~WHEN THE STRANGE THING ABOUT THESE FIRE FIGHTS~~ SOON THE ENEMY WAS OVERWHELMED AND PINNED DOWN. THROUGH A COMBINATION OF GUN RUNS AND A 500LB BOMB THE ENEMY WAS DESTROYED. WE EXPERINCED _NO_ ~~CAS~~ CAUSUALTIES THAT DAY, A FACT & CREDIT TO JESUS AND JESUS ALONE.

Zee shitter

PTE
A moment Il Never forget
is when are multipole was
Down at checkpoint 32 and
we had Just HAD a re/supply
with parcels and mail and
I was sat in the cooking area
with a few of the lads. When
are platoon commander come in
asking if we had good mail
later on that night he told
a few of us that his Girlfriend
had sent him a dear JOHN
letter (finishing Him) all the blokes
looked at him and burst out
laughing.

PTE

A moment Il Never Forget
Is When are multipule was
Down at checkpoint 32 and
we had Just HAO a re/supply
With parcels and mail and
I was Sat In the Cooking area
with a few of the Lads. When
are platoon Commander Come in
asking if we had good mail
Later on that night he told
a few of us that his Girlfriend
had sent him a dear John
letter (Finishing Him) all the blokes
looked at him and burst out
laughing.

War is a dirty business

I will not allow myself
to read or even look at
glossy magazines while
I am in Afganistan, war
is a dirty business in
both senses of the word
and it both Annoyes
me and frustrates me to
see page after page of
women splashed accross
the Magazines and So
Called Celebs who have
no idea of what is being
or done accross here living
in a dirty and deprived
but real environment.

I will not allow myself to read or even look at glossy Magazines while I am in Afganistan, war is a dirty buissness in both Senses of the word and it both Annoyes me and frustrates me to See page after page of women Splashed accross the Magazines and So Called Celebs who have no Idea of what is being done accross here living in a dirty and deprived but real Environment.

My brother's death

FOB KNK 27-01

One more day and my tour is over. New friends
among gurkhas, mercians and guardsmen.
Strong frienship with my buddy Allan.
And accepted my brother death. The primary
mission of my tour.
Pround of having served with british troops.

WO2 FRANK (DK)

"IT'S BETTER TO LIVE ONE DAY AS A LION
THAN 100 YEARS AS A SHEEP"

FOB KWK 27-01

One more day and my tour is over. New friends among gurkhas, mercians and guardsmen.
Strong friendship with my buddy Allan.
And accepted my brother death. The primary mission of my tour.
Proud of having served with british troops.

WO2 FRANK (DK)

"IT'S BETTER TO LIVE ONE DAY AS A LION THAN 100 YEARS AS A SHEEP" :)

Yummy!

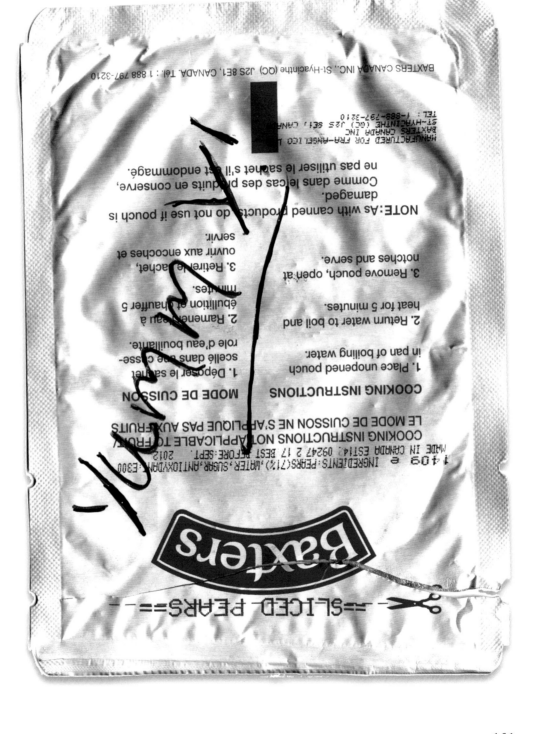

Fuck off and stop shooting at me

When we first got
To afgan IN The first contact
we were scared
The second we were exited
The Third we were used to
IT. The forth we couldent
be arsed
Coming close to RNR I
wish the Taliban would
fuck off and STOP shooting
at me.

W/H 1IG
Manchester

When we first got
To afgan to the first contact
we were scared
The second we were exited
The third we were used to
it. The forth we couldent
be arsed
coming close to RnR I
wish The Taliban would
fuck off and STOP Shooting
at me.

w/H 1TG
Manchester.

I owe you a pint I think

Another morning Patrol in NADI-ALI in
November 2010
and another contact with Taliban
Fighters, we were engaged by multiple
Firing Points and the rounds were
getting closer and closer, we
called motars and 105mm's in
with almost no effect, things were
getting worse, as taliban fighters
were now boxing around us and
rounds were coming from the
Front side and behind, I thought
It was It, any second and a
round would hit me. Then to my
Thanks the sound of a apache
was overhead and even better
the beatiful Purr of the 30mm
cannon was singing to us all.
A.H was engaging taliban 80m
In front of me with Dirt and
Branches being sprayed everywhere.
The A.H Truely saved our ass that
day and still we never met the
Pilot. But if he's reading this I Guess
cheers mate I owe you a Pint I think

Another Morning Patrol in NADI-ALE in November 2010 and another contact with Taliban Fighters, we were engaged by multiple Firing points and the rounds were getting closer and closer, we called motors and 105mm's In with almost no effect, things were getting worse, as taliban Fighters were now boxing around us and rounds were coming from the front Side and behind, I thought It was It, any Second and a round would hit me. Then to my Thanks the Sound of a apache was overhead and even better the beectiful Purr of the 30mm canon was singing to us all. A.H was engageing taliban 80 m in front of me with Dirt and Branches being sprayed everywhere. The A.H Truely Saved our ass that day and still we never met the pilot. But if he's reading this I Guess cheers mate I owe you a Pint I think

I have seldom felt so alone or so scared

1/

ON OPERATION SAFE VILLAGE TO CLEAR
THE VILLAGE OF CHAR-COUCHA OF IED'S.
WE USED THE BRIMSTONE TEAMS TO CLEAR
THE IED'S WITH (ATO) DURING THE DAY
AND PATROLED OUT OF TEMPORARY CP'S
AT NIGHT TO ENSURE THE ENEMY DID
NOT RE-SEED IED'S IN BEHIND OR
AROUND US, THUS ENSURING THE CLEARED
AREAS REMAINED SO. DURING THE NIGHT
I WOULD LEAD PROWLER PATROLS OF
ISAF AND ANA TROOPS INTO AND AROUND
THE CLEARED COMPOUNDS. ON ONE SUCH
NIGHT IN LATE JAN 11 I LEAD ONE
PARACHUTE REGIMENT TOM AND X3 ANA
SGT'S INTO AN ALLYWAY WHICH HAD
ALREADY CLAIMED THE LIFE OF A
BRITISH OFFICER NEAR THE SOUTH

V

On Operation Safe Village to clear the village of Char-Concha of IED's. We used the Brimstone teams to clear the IED's with (ATO) during the day and patroled out of temporary CP's at night to ensure the enemy did not re-seed IED's in behind or around us, thus ensuring the cleared areas remained so. During the night I would lead Prowler patrols of ISAF and ANA troops into and around the cleared compounds. On one such night in late Jan 11 I lead one Parachute Regiment Tom and x3 ANA Sgt's into an allyway which had already claimed the life of a British officer near the south

2/

CLUSTER OF COMPOUNDS NEAR PB1.
IT WAS A VERY CANNELLIZED ROUTE
WITH HIGH MUD WALLS WITH GAPS
CAUSED BY WAR DAMAGE AND HEAVY
FIGHTING WITH AN OPEN FIELD TO THE
LEFT AND COMPOUNDS BEYOND. IT WAS
DARK AND EERIE AND WE SHONE WHITE
LIGHT FROM OUR LLM'S TO SEE THE
GROUND SIGN. WE PASSED THE JUNCTION
WHERE THE BRITISH LT HAD BEEN
KILLED BY A (VO IED) AND COULD STILL
SEE THE CREATOR, SENDING A CHILL UP
OUR SPINES. THE ALLYWAY LEAD IN
2 DIRECTIONS FROM THEN ON. WE
WENT LEFT TOWARDS ANOTHER COMPOUND
THAT WE KNEW WAS OCCUPIED WHICH
MADE US FEEL BETTER UNTIL WE
CAME TO ANOTHER CREATOR IN THE
GROUND WHERE BRIMSTONE BLEW

2/ CLUSTER OF COMPOUNDS NEAR PB 1.
IT WAS A VERY CANELLIZED ROUTE
WITH HIGH MUD WALLS WITH GAPS
CAUSED BY WAR DAMAGE AND HEAVY
FIGHTING WITH AN OPEN FIELD TO THE
LEFT AND COMPOUNDS BEYOND. IT WAS
DARK AND EERIE AND WE SHONE WHITE
LIGHT FROM OUR LLM'S TO SEE THE
GROUND SIGN. WE PASSED THE JUNCTION
WHERE THE BRITISH LT HAD BEEN
KILLED BY A (VOIED) AND COULD STILL
SEE THE CREATOR, SENDING A CHILL UP
OUR SPINES. THE ALLY WAY LEAD IN
2 DIRECTIONS FROM THEN ON.. WE
WENT LEFT TOWARDS ANOTHER COMPOUND
THAT WE KNEW WAS OCCUPIED WHICH
MADE US FEEL BETTER UNTIL WE
CAME TO ANOTHER CREATOR IN THE
GROUND WHERE BRIMSTONE BLEW

3/ UP ANOTHER DEVICE FOUND
THAT VERY DAY – THEN BANG!
A SNIPER. IT WAS VERY LOUD AND
WE ALL INSTINCTIVELY HIT THE DECK.
WE WHERE PINNED DOWN. I TASKED
REVIVER, THE IR BALLON TO LOOK
INTO DEPTH FROM CP LAMAR.
IT PICKED UP A HEAT SOURCE FROM
COMPOUND 17. I HAD 3 MEN WHOM
DID NOT SHARE MY LANGUAGE AND
A YOUNG PARATROOPER LOOKING AT
ME FOR DIRECTION/LEADERSHIP. TO
GO FORWARD COULD HAVE MEANT
DEATH OR A COMMAND WIRE IED.
TO GO BACK DOWN THE ALLY COULD
HAVE MEANT DEATH BY (SAF).
I HAD TO MAKE A HASTY DECISION

3/
UP ANOTHER DEVICE FOUND
THAT VERY DAY - THEN BANG!
A SNIPER. IT WAS VERY LOUD AND
WE ALL INSTINCTIVELY HIT THE DECK.
WE WHERE PINNED DOWN. I TASKED
REVIVER, THE IR BALLON TO LOOK
INTO DEPTH FROM CP LAMAR.
IT PICKED UP A HEAT SOURCE FROM
COMPOUND 17. I HAD 3 MEN WHOM
DID NOT SHARE MY LANGUAGE AND
A YOUNG PARATROOPER LOOKING AT
ME FOR DIRECTION/LEADERSHIP. TO
GO FORWARD COULD HAVE MEANT
DEATH OR A COMMAND WIRE IED.
TO GO BACK DOWN THE ALLY COULD
HAVE MEANT DEATH BY (SAF).
I HAD TO MAKE A HASTY DECISION

4/

I HAVE SELDOM FELT SO
ALONE IN MY LIFE, OR SO
SCARED. WE LEAP-FROGGED
OUT OF THAT ALLY WAY OF DEATH
AND THE (ANA) INTELLIGENCE
WAS RIGHT - THE ENEMY WHERE
DOING THEIR OWN PATROLS IN
THE AREA. THAT NIGHT.
CSGT
ROBERT LYTTLE
1ST BN IRISH GUARDS
ADVISOR 34
PB 1 NES(S)

4/
I HAVE SELDOM FELT SO
ALONE IN MY LIFE, OR SO
SCARED, WE LEAP-FROGGED
OUT OF THAT ALLYWAY OF DEATH
BUT THE (ANA) INTELLIGENCE
WAS RIGHT – THE ENEMY WHERE
DOING THEIR OWN PATROLS IN
THE AREA THAT NIGHT.
CSGT
ROBERT LYTTLE
1st BN IRISH GUARDS
ADVISOR 34
PB 1 NES(S)

Respect

ISAF helps ANA.
Afghans and Afghanistan
and they respect Afghans.
and Islam.

بریښنا مل نوکی اول محترم انه ورقه څلارم

اردوی ملی افغانستان

ایشان له اردوی ملی سره همکاری ئی

امریکی ګی اول اردوی ملی سره

نظو به انتقاد ننګه اوهمکاری کوی

اوله ایشان نخه زمونږ نه حالوات

وادی می دوی د افغانانو دویی

امذهب هرپر احترام کوی

محترم انه

Smudge had lost both legs

Out on my first tour of Afghanistan as part of the Counter IED Task force, our first couple of weeks were very quiet. We got moved from our original location in PB3 NEs(S) up to PB1 to clear a route down to CP LAMAR. The search teams were out on the ground one morning nearing the end of the search task, when Spr ▮▮▮▮ stepped on an IED. I was in my tent at the time on a short notice to move if anything was found by the search team. I heard the explosion, it sounded like it came from exactly where the guys were searching. We moved down as quickly as we could to help out but by the time we had got to the CP the guys were already back in having done an excellent First Aid Job. It was clear to see that Smudge had lost both legs and the team were very upset. It was a horrible thing to happen especially at the beginning of the 6 months. I will always remember the look on his face.

Out on my first tour of Afghanistan as part of the Counter IED Task force, our first couple of weeks were very quiet. We got moved from our original location in PB3 NES(s) up to PB1 to clear a route down to CP LAMAR. The search teams were out on the ground one morning nearing the end of the search task, when Spr ███████ stepped on an IED. I was in my tent at the time on a short notice to move if anything was found by the search team. I heard the explosion, it sounded like it came from exactly where the guys were searching. We moved down as quickly as we could to help out but by the time we had got to the CP the guys were already back in having done an excellent First Aid Job. It was clear to see that Smudge had lost both legs and the team were very upset. It was a horrible thing to happen especially at the beginning of the 6 months. I will always remember the look on his face.

A beautiful walk in some forgotten world

This could be a beautiful walk in some forgotten world that time has merely neglected, but then a burst of reality strafes across my platoon and the rounds smash into the ground around us.

Everything clicks into place:
  Why the endless platoon attacks
          across Brecon.
  Why the countless estimate tasks.
  Why the ceaseless physical tasks.

Your mind clicks into a gear that you never knew you had, and you bark orders like your life depends on it...and GUESS WHAT IT DOES! AND YOU CAN'T HELP BUT SMILE TO YOURSELF FOR THE LAST 18 MONTHS OF TRAINING HAS WORKED.

FOB KNK   A RED ARSE

This could be a 'beautiful walk in some forgotten world that time has merely neglected, but then a burst of reality swafes across my platoon and the rounds smash into the ground around us.

Everything clicks into place:
  why the endless platoon attacks
      across Brecon.
  why the countless estimate tasks.
  why the ceaseless physical tasks.

Your mind clicks into a gear that you never knew you had, and you bark orders like your life depends on it ... and GUESS WHAT IT DOES! AND YOU CAN'T HELP BUT SMILE TO YOURSELF FOR THE LAST 18 MONTHS OF TRAINING HAS WORKED.

FOB KNK   A RED ARSE

all gave some
and some gave all.

Our task was to help Afghanistan find long-term stability so it would never again become a cradle for international terrorism. Working with others, we sought to give the people the confidence to stand up to the Taliban and to place their trust in the new Afghan Government.

Afghanistan is a captivating land; harsh and beautiful. We were there as the balance was shifting in favour of the Afghan security forces. Progress was delivered through humility and careful judgement, and it demanded an unrelenting fight against those who sought to drag the country back to its ugly past. More than 450 British service personnel have paid the ultimate sacrifice during this campaign. Of those whom were there, all gave some and some gave all.

James Chiswell
Task Force Commander, OP HERRICK 13.

178

Our task was to help Afghanistan find long-term stability so it would never again become a cradle for international terrorism. Working with others, we sought to give the people the confidence to stand up to the Taliban and to place their trust in the new Afghan Government.

Afghanistan is a captivating land; harsh and beautiful. We were there as the balance was shifting in favour of the Afghan security forces. Progress was delivered through humility and careful judgement, and if demanded an unrelenting fight against those who sought to drag the country back to its ugly past.

More than 450 British service personnel have paid the ultimate sacrifice during this campaign.

Of those whom were there, all gave some and some gave all.

James Chiswell
Task Force Commander, Op HERRICK 13.

Honesty

It's the honesty of these stories that makes them important

The last photo of me with legs

When I was in Afghanistan in 2011 an artist visited the front line – from what I remember he was tall, unassuming, pleasant. Our tour was in transit. Four months in and a fortnight away from my R&R. That notion of R&R was slowly creeping into my consciousness, I couldn't help it. I am human after all. This tall artist handed me a postcard and said "Here you are, write down anything you like about what it's like to be here". "Anything?" I replied. "Yes, anything that comes into your head, anything you feel".

Early in the morning three days later, while on a fighting patrol, I trod on an IED. It took my feet away in a couple of tenths of a second turning them into some sort of mist and threw me what could have been 10-12 feet in the air. It was a jolt to the system. Many of the words I'd learnt to talk to the Afghan people I could never remember. Not because of any neurological injury. They simply got blew out of me. Writing my thoughts and feelings on a postcard was like it never even happened.

Three years later I met this artist again and we talked. I have a beard now and I'm less intense. I recalled that he joined me on sentry duty that night - a moment on a roof of a compound in Afghanistan while my mates slept beneath me all came back to me. We talked about music and that it was the space between the notes that made the music. Perhaps I existed in the space between when we are being attacked and not attacked. The space is real. There's stuff there. All this led to the emergence of a photograph he had taken of me in Afghanistan in 2011 – the last ever photo taken of me with legs. Derek, thank you for the memory.

Colum McGeown's story p33

Colum McGeown, April 2014

Glossary

105 mm	The shell from a light gun
1 R Irish	1st Battalion, The Royal Irish Regiment
1IG	1st Battalion, Irish Guards
2 PARA	2nd Battalion, The Parachute Regiment
2 i/c	Second in command
2Lt	Rank of 2nd Lieutenant
3 PARA	3rd Battalion, The Parachute Regiment
A10	Close air support aircraft
AK47	7.62mm short cartridge rifle
ANA	Afghan National Army
ANP	Afghan National Police
AO	Area of Operations
Apache	Attack helicopter (AH)
ATO	Ammunition Technical Officer
BDR	Bahadur, a patrol base in Helmand
BCR	Battle Casualty Replacement
BN	Battalion
Brews	Tea/coffee
Brize	RAF Brize Norton in the UK
Bty	Battery
Camp Bastion	The main British military base in Afghanistan
CAPT	Rank of Captain
CASEVAC	Casualty Evacuation
Cat A	Classification of seriousness of wound meaning 'critically injured'
Chinook	Twin propeller helicopter
Chopper	Helicopter
CIED	Counter IED
COIN	Counter-Insurgency
Compound	House, living area
Contact	Military language for being attacked

Coy	Company
CP	Check Point
CPL	Rank of Corporal
C/S	Callsign for a military unit
CSGT	Rank of Colour Sergeant
CSM	Rank of Company Sergeant Major
Double amp	Amputee with two limbs lost
D Coy	D Company
EOD	Explosive Ordnance Disposal
Faugh-a-Ballagh	'Clear the Way', Regimental motto of the Royal Irish Regiment
FOB	Forward Operating Base
Frag	Fragmentation from, for example, a grenade
FSG	Fire Support Group
GDSM	Guardsman
GPMG	General Purpose Machine Gun
Green Zone	Fertile strip of irrigated land either side of the Helmand river and its tributaries
Helmand	A Province in Afghanistan
Herrick	The codename under which all British operations in the war in Afghanistan have been conducted since 2002
HLS	Helicopter Landing Site
ICOM	Intercepted Communications
IED	Improvised Explosive Device
Illum	Illumination flares
INS	Insurgents
ISAF	International Security Assistance Force
ISO	Shipping container
JAV	Javelin, medium range anti-tank guided weapon
Kinetic	Euphemism for military action
L/CPL	Rank of Lance Corporal

LASM	Light Anti-Structures Missile, rocket launcher
LBdr	Rank of Lance Bombadier
LLM	Laser Light Module illumination
LMG	Light Machine Gun
LN	Local national
Lt	Rank of Lieutenant
MC	Military Cross medal
MERT	Medical Emergency Response Team
MIST	Acronym for an injury report covering: M- Mechanism of injury; I- Injury or illness sustained; S- Symptoms and vital signs T- Treatments given
MSST	Military Stabilisation Support Team
MMG	Medium Machine Gun
MWD	Military Working Dog
Multiple	Military unit
Nad Ali	A District of Helmand
NATO	North Atlantic Treaty Organisation
OC	Officer Commanding
Op	Operation
Op Massive	Fitness training
Op Minimise	A blackout of phones, email, text and internet communications across Afghanistan when there is a Category A British Casualty or fatality
PAX	Person
PB	Patrol Base
PKM	Russian-made rifle
PLT	Platoon
PNR	Pioneer
Pte	Rank of Private
QRF	Quick Reaction Force
Quis Separabit (QS)	Latin for 'Who shall separate us?'
R&R	Rest and Recuperation

RAVC	Royal Army Veterinary Corps
RE	Royal Engineers
Recce	Reconnaissance
Reg	Regiment
REME	Royal Mechanical and Electrical Engineers
RGR	Ranger
RHA	Royal Horse Artillery
Rounds	Bullets/ammunition
RPG	Rocket-Propelled Grenade
RSOI	Reception, Staging and Onward Movement Integration
SA80	Standard-issue British Army rifle
SAF	Small arms fire, eg. Rifle
Saidabad	A town in Helmand
Sangar	Small fortified position
SF	Special Forces
Sgt	Rank of Sergeant
Spectemur Agendo	Latin for 'Let us be judged by our acts'
SPR	Sapper
Stag	Sentry duty
TA	Territorial Army
Terp	Interpreter
Toms	Paratroopers
TMWDSU	Theatre Military Working Dog Support Unit
UGL	Underslung grenade launcher
Vallon	Mine detector
VO IED	Victim operated IED
WO2	Rank of Warrant Officer Class 2

Acknowledgements

Afghan National Army
Agence France-Presse
16 Air Assault Brigade
The Irish Guards
The Royal Irish Regiment
The Parachute Regiment
The Arts Council
BBC
Steve Biddle
The Big Ideas Collective
CNN
Major-General James Chiswell CBE MC
Combat Stress
The family of David Dalzell
frieze magazine
Bear Grylls
The Huffington Post
Imperial War Museum
The Independent
All those who supported through Indiegogo
Colum McGeown
Middlesbrough Institute of Modern Art
Ministry of Defence
The Mirror
Russell Cotes Art Gallery and Museum
War, Literature and the Arts

About the artist

Derek Eland is an artist and former paratrooper. He has a degree in Politics and a masters degree in Contemporary Fine Art. In 2011 he spent a month on the front line in Afghanistan as an official war artist. His work has been exhibited internationally and short-listed for a number of awards. He lives in the UK and this is his first book.
www.derekeland.com